EVERY SINGLE CENT

FINANCIAL GUIDE FOR SINGLE ADULTS

WORKBOOK

LARRY BURKETT

WITH BRENDA ARMSTRONG

All Scripture quotations are from the *NEW AMERICAN STANDARD BIBLE* (updated edition),
© 1960, 1962, 1963, 1968, 1971, 1972, 1973, 1975, 1977, 1995
by the Lockman Foundation. Used by permission.

Edited by Adeline Griffith, Crown Financial Ministries

Library of Congress Cataloging-in-Publication Data

Burkett, Larry.

     Every Single Cent

ISBN # 1-56427-064-5

    1.   Single adults—United States—Finance, Personal.

12-01

Printed in the United States of America.

TABLE OF CONTENTS

INTRODUCTION

Dealing with finances is difficult for most people. The idea of budgeting may make them nervous. Although budgeting decisions can cause arguments in many families, two heads usually are better than one. Often, one person is a spender and the other a saver. Budgeting for single adults can be especially challenging because they don't have anyone else with whom to share the decision-making responsibilities. If a single is a spender, no one counter-balances it. It's the same with singles who save. This hinders making a balanced budget. Another hindrance for single adults is the fear that a budget will restrict their social spending and limit their ability to interact with others.

The above problems represent some of the most common faced by single adults. However, their financial situations vary widely.

✦ Some older single adults live on small fixed incomes.

✦ Many younger single adults have established careers but have amassed school loans or credit debt to achieve that.

✦ Single adults in their 40s and 50s may fear retirement because they aren't prepared financially.

✦ Other single adults are facing the possibility of caring for elderly parents.

Although each group has a unique set of circumstances, there are principles that apply in most of them. In this workbook, we have compiled some of the basics that will help alleviate fears and meet the needs of single adults who are older than college age and not raising or supporting children.

No matter what your circumstances are, as a single adult you need not be afraid of budgeting. A budget is simply a spending plan you create to cover your expenses and is not as restrictive as you might believe. A budget actually relieves the worry, guilt, frustration, and anxiety that uncontrolled spending presents. Although it takes discipline to stick to a budget, it actually frees more money to invest in the kingdom of God and for your future.

Crown Financial Ministries has many other resources available to help people learn biblical truths about finances that apply during different times of their lives.

✦ *Making Ends Meet, Budgeting Made Easy* is a very easy-to-use, first workbook for people who have never budgeted before or who may not have many financial responsibilities.

✦ *Money Before Marriage* is for couples engaged to be married.

✦ *Money in Marriage* is for married couples.

✦ *Money Management for College Students* fits the needs of young single adults.

✦ *The Financial Guide for the Single Parent* book and workbook are available to help single parents face their budeting problems and fears.

✦ This workbook for single adults has been adapted from *The Financial Planning Workbook* by Larry Burkett.

Special Studies

✦ *Crown Small Group Study* can be used by a church only in a small-group setting with at least two trained small group leaders. It is not available for individual sale.

✦ *Discovering God's Way of Handling Money* (video series, workbook, and leader's guide) is designed for individual use or in a Sunday school setting or weekend seminar.

For more information about these exciting tools to help develop financial freedom, have your pastor or minister of education contact us.

To receive our monthly newsletter or to order any of our resources, write to Crown Financial Ministries, PO Box 100, Gainesville GA 30503-0100; call (800) 722-1976; or visit our Web site at www.crown.org.

GETTING STARTED

There may be a lot of reasons why we need to learn how to manage our money. The most important reason is because it is important to God. His Word reveals a lot about how we are to handle our resources.

The Twelve Biblical Principles of Money Management

Principle #1: God owns everything, and we are simply His managers or stewards.

Biblical truths: *"The earth is the Lord's, and all it contains, the world, and those who dwell in it"* (Psalm 24:1).

"By Him all things were created, both in the heavens and on earth" (Colossians 1:16).

It's a mistake to think that we own anything. When we begin to realize that God owns all we have, we have begun to understand the first principle of stewardship.

Principle #2: True wealth consists of all that God entrusts to us, including spiritual blessings, family, health, work, and material goods.

Biblical truth: *"It is the blessing of the Lord that makes rich, and He adds no sorrow to it"* (Proverbs 10:22).

Our jobs, ingenuity, talents, and abilities only provide for us because God gave us those gifts. Our trust must be placed in the Provider. If we trust only in what those gifts provide, we will lose heart when circumstances change.

Principle #3: God's presence brings hope, even in extreme financial situations.

Biblical truth: *"Now may the God of hope fill you with all joy and peace in believing, so that you will abound in hope by the power of the Holy Spirit"* (Romans 15:13).

Once we trust that God is the provider, we can trust Him when things change. Our hope is built on a constant source—not a changeable circumstance.

Principle #4: God creates each of us with certain personality strengths that impact our approach to money management.

Biblical truth: *"I will give thanks to You, for I am fearfully and wonderfully made; wonderful are Your works, and my soul knows it very well"* (Psalm 139:14).

God designed each one of us in a unique way to fulfill His purposes. Success is operating in the gifts and talents that God has given us. Sometimes we move far from His design, but it is still resident in us. We can get back on track by examining the talents and abilities He has given us and taking steps in that direction.

Principle #5: Financial bondage is the natural consequence of misusing the resources God has entrusted to us.

Biblical truths: *"The rich rules over the poor, and the borrower becomes the lender's slave"* (Proverbs 22:7).

"He said to them, 'Beware, and be on your guard against every form of greed; for not even when one has an abundance does his life consist of his possessions' " (Luke 12:15).

"The wicked borrows and does not pay back, but the righteous is gracious and gives" (Psalm 37:21).

Indebtedness can result from greed or circumstances. Whatever the source, indebtedness leads to bondage because you aren't free to use your resources. They now belong to someone else.

Principle #6: Financial freedom results from committing all aspects of life to God and by faithfully obeying His principles.

Biblical truths: *"It was for freedom that Christ set us free; therefore keep standing firm and do not be subject again to a yoke of slavery"* (Galatians 5:1).

"Where your treasure is, there your heart will be also" (Matthew 6:21).

Principle #7: Preplanning is a strategic first step toward responsible money management.

Biblical truths: *"Prepare your work outside and make it ready for yourself in the field; afterwards, then, build your house"* (Proverbs 24:27).

"All things must be done properly and in an orderly manner" (1 Corinthians 14:40).

It is often said that the best defense is a good offense. Why wait until trouble appears to begin to plan? We must begin to look at our circumstances realistically.

Principle #8: Establishing a budget enables us to live according to God's priorities.

Biblical truths: *"The plans of the diligent lead surely to advantage, but everyone who is hasty comes surely to poverty"* (Proverbs 21:5).

"The prudent sees the evil and hides himself, but the naive go on, and are punished for it" (Proverbs 22:3).

Principle #9: Long-range planning helps us to discern God's fundamental purpose and direction in life.

Biblical truths: *"Which one of you, when he wants to build a tower, does not first sit down and calculate the cost to see if he has enough to complete it? Otherwise, when he has laid a foundation and is not able to finish, all who observe it begin to ridicule him, saying, 'This man began to build and was not able to finish' "* (Luke 14:28-30).

"There is precious treasure and oil in the dwelling of the wise, but a foolish man swallows it up" (Proverbs 21:20).

Principle #10: Following biblical principles of giving reflects God's love and financial priorities.

Biblical truths: *"You will be enriched in everything for all liberality, which through us is producing thanksgiving to God"* (2 Corinthians 9:11).

"Now this I say, he who sows sparingly will also reap sparingly, and he who sows bountifully will also reap bountifully" (2 Corinthians 9:6).

There are people in need all around us. If we are faithful with what God has given us and learn to live a moderate lifestyle, we often have the resources to help others in need.

Principle #11: Contentment comes from understanding and accepting God's sovereign plan for living.

Biblical truths: *"Make sure that your character is free from the love of money, being content with what you have; for He Himself has said, 'I will never desert you, nor will I ever forsake you' "* (Hebrews 13:5).

Principle #8: Establishing a budget enables us to live according to God's priorities.

Biblical truths: *"The plans of the diligent lead surely to advantage, but everyone who is hasty comes surely to poverty"* (Proverbs 21:5).

"The prudent sees the evil and hides himself, but the naive go on, and are punished for it" (Proverbs 22:3).

Principle #9: Long-range planning helps us to discern God's fundamental purpose and direction in life.

Biblical truths: *"Which one of you, when he wants to build a tower, does not first sit down and calculate the cost to see if he has enough to complete it? Otherwise, when he has laid a foundation and is not able to finish, all who observe it begin to ridicule him, saying, 'This man began to build and was not able to finish'"* (Luke 14:28-30).

"There is precious treasure and oil in the dwelling of the wise, but a foolish man swallows it up" (Proverbs 21:20).

Principle #10: Following biblical principles of giving reflects God's love and financial priorities.

Biblical truths: *"You will be enriched in everything for all liberality, which through us is producing thanksgiving to God"* (2 Corinthians 9:11).

Needs	Wants	Desires
These are the purchases necessary to provide your basic requirements, such as Food, Clothing, Housing, Medical, and others (1 Timothy 6:8)	Wants involve choices about the quality of goods to be used. Designer clothes versus work clothes, steak versus hambuger, a new car versus a used car. First Peter 3:3-4 gives a point of reference for determining wants in a Christian's life.	These are choices that can be made according to God's plan and only out of surplus funds after all other obligations have been met (1 John 2:15-16).

Obstacles to Good Planning

- ✦ No one to balance financial decisions.

- ✦ The need to spend on socializing.

- ✦ Social pressures to own more "things."

- ✦ The attitude that "more is better" regardless of the cost.

- ✦ Using credit to delay necessary decisions.

- ✦ Having no surplus available to cope with rising prices and unexpected expenses.

- ✦ Offsetting increases by spending more money.

The attitudes supporting these obstacles can create a real problem because they lead to . . .

The Danger Point

. . . when income barely equals outgo.

Breaking even is not a *living point* but a *decision point.* If all the income is consumed in monthly expenses and something unusual happens, such as an unpaid medical leave or the automobile breaking down, the result is additional indebtedness.

A decision is necessary at this point: **MAKE MORE MONEY OR SPEND LESS.**

Ideally, this decision would be made before external pressures left few alternatives. Unfortunately, when the pressure comes on, the credit card comes out. The result is a debt that cannot be paid. This limits the alternatives, and the solution is usually only treating the "symptoms." Some typical "solutions" are bill consolidation, loans, additional credit, second mortgages, borrowing from relatives or friends, or a second job. Those may provide temporary relief; but, unfortunately, since only the symptom has been treated, the problem still exits. It's only a matter of time until the symptoms reappear.

It is obviously better to cut expenses than to attempt to increase income. Unfortunately, it is also painful. The key? *Commitment.*

Recognize the Divisions of Income
(See Figure 1.1 on page 8.)

- ■ The *first* part belongs to God.

    It is returned to Him as a tithe in recognition that He owns all that we have. We are merely stewards. *"Will a man rob God? Yet you are robbing Me! But you say, 'How have we robbed You?' In tithes and offerings"* (Malachi 3:8).

■ The *government* wants its share.

"He said to them, 'Then render to Caesar the things that are Caesar's; and to God the things that are God's' " (Matthew 22:21).

The portion available after tithe and taxes is called **Net Spendable Income.**

■ *Basic needs* come next.

"Storing up for themselves the treasure of a good foundation for the future, so that they may take hold of that which is life indeed" (1 Timothy 6:19).

■ God says to pay your *debts.*

"The wicked borrows and does not pay back, but the righteous is gracious and gives" (Psalm 37:21).

■ Faithful management will yield a fifth portion—*a surplus.*

The creation of a **surplus** should be a major goal for every Christian. It is the surplus that allows us to respond to the needs of others. *"At this present time your abundance being a supply for their need, so that their abundance also may become a supply for your need, that there may be equality"* (2 Corinthians 8:14).

Even if you are not in debt, to maximize the surplus your finances should be budget controlled.

In addition to responding to the needs of others, it's the surplus that provides the flexibility to meet emergencies without credit. That surplus also can be used to invest and multiply your assets.

Where Do I Start?

Starting a budget is just like starting on a trip. You cannot set a course without first determining where you are.

Step one—The budget

What is the present level of spending?

Step two—Budget goals

Establish the "ideal" budget. In actuality, few people ever reach the ideal, but it is possible to establish the "now" condition by reviewing the ideal.

This trip (of establishing a budget) will consist of comparing the present spending level with a guideline for balanced spending. The comparison will point out where adjustments should be made.

Once the budget is established, a control system must be incorporated that will keep spending on the "road." The system must be able to sound the alarm **before** overspending occurs.

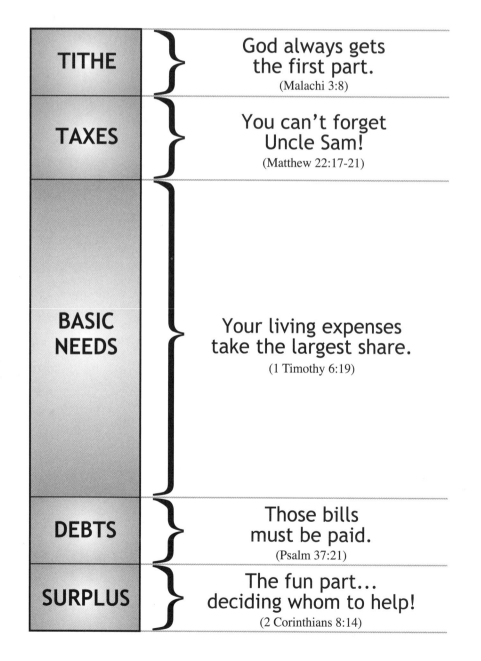

TITHE — God always gets the first part. (Malachi 3:8)

TAXES — You can't forget Uncle Sam! (Matthew 22:17-21)

BASIC NEEDS — Your living expenses take the largest share. (1 Timothy 6:19)

DEBTS — Those bills must be paid. (Psalm 37:21)

SURPLUS — The fun part... deciding whom to help! (2 Corinthians 8:14)

Figure 1.1

There Are Road Hazards

Discouragement

To complete the trip, one must keep going. A major problem is to develop a budget and then to not follow it.

Legalism

Another problem is becoming legalistic and inflexible. Then the budget becomes a problem instead of a solution. Incidentally, being legalistic seems to occur at the same time the money runs out. If a road is blocked we usually have to take another route to get to where we are going. Remain flexible to necessary changes.

Overcorrecting

When the money gets tight, the tendency is to eliminate clothes, entertainment, food, and other "expendables." That creates a pressure that is often relieved by over-spending in other areas.

Misuse of an abundance

Financial bondage can result from a lack of money and overspending; but, it can also be caused from the misuse of an abundance of money. Some people have enough money to be undisciplined and get away with it (financially speaking). But true financial freedom requires us to be good stewards (Matthew 24:45). That is only possible with self-discipline. It also will require some sacrifice.

A good plan requires **action** and **discipline** to work. The first action is prayer. Ask God to help you face your financial situation realistically. Then ask Him to give you wisdom to make the necessary changes.

Begin now!

WHERE ARE YOU?

Determining Monthly Income and Expenses

The Present Condition

On the monthly Income and Expenses form (Figure 2.1 on page 19), compare actual monthly expenses with monthly income to determine your present spending. (Note: You may need to keep a diary of expenses for a few months before you can accurately determine actual monthly expenses.)

To determine living costs, consider what represents a reasonable standard of living at your present income level. You will see that you need to make adjustments in some areas. However, reasonable, not total, sacrifices are necessary. When you set up your new budget, do not eliminate areas like personal spending, clothes, savings, entertainment, and recreation.

When you set up your new budget, be sure to include a reasonable amount for personal spending.

Determining Income Per Month

List all gross income (income before deductions) in the "Income Per Month" section on the Monthly Income and Expenses Sheet. Don't forget to include commissions, bonuses, tips, and interest earned that will be received over the next 12 months.

When income consists totally or partially of commissions or other fluctuating resources, average the amount you receive each year and divide by 12. Use a low yearly average, not a high average.

If you are paid on a weekly or biweekly basis, take the total yearly income and divide by 12.

Business expenses reimbursements should not be considered income. Avoid the trap of using expense money to buffer spending or the result will be an indebtedness that cannot be paid.

What Is "Net Spendable Income"?

Net spendable income is the portion available for spending. Some of your income does not belong to you and therefore cannot be spent.

Category 1

The Tithe: Since the term *tithe* means "a tenth," we will assume that you give 10 percent of your total income to God. For a detailed discussion on the tithe, see *Your Finances in Changing Times* by Larry Burkett, published by Moody Press; chapter 10, "Sharing—God's Way."

Category 2

Taxes: Federal withholding, Social Security, and state and local taxes also must be deducted from gross income. Self-employed individuals must not forget to set aside money for quarterly prepayment on taxes. Beware of the tendency to treat unpaid tax money as windfall profit.

Other Deductions: Payroll deductions or insurance, medical or child care deductions, savings deductions, debt payments, bonds, stock programs, retirement, and union dues can be handled in either of two ways.

1. Treat them as deductions from gross income, the same as income taxes.

2. Include them in spendable income and deduct them from the proper category. This is preferred because it provides a more accurate picture of where the money is being spent.

Net Spendable Income is gross income minus tithe and taxes.

> ### Example
>
> *A deduction is being made for savings. This amount should be considered part of income and the expense should show under "Savings" for that amount. This method makes it easier to see the overall effect the deduction has on your budget.*

How Is Net Spendable Income Being Spent?

Category 3

Housing: All monthly expenses necessary to maintain your residence, including all utilities, phone, home or rental insurance, membership or association fees, maintenance fees or repairs, and real estate taxes if applicable. The amount for utilities should be an average monthly amount for the past 12 months. If you have not lived very long at your present residence, ask the utility company for an average for your unit or house.

If you are sharing housing, include all the expenses you pay or your portion of the expenses.

If you own a home and cannot establish an accurate maintenance expense, use 5 percent of the monthly mortgage payment. Older homes may need a higher percentage rate.

Category 4

Food Expenses: This covers all grocery expenses, including paper goods, pet food, and nonfood products normally purchased at grocery stores. Include extra trips for bread and milk. **Do not include eating out,** which is included in the Entertainment category.

It is common for single adults to purchase expensive convenience foods since they eat most of their meals alone. Many singles have cut this expense by cooking family-size meals once or twice a week and freezing them in individual containers for future use. They should be dated and eaten within three months. Sometimes singles share meals with other single friends and take turns preparing meals.

Category 5

Transportation Expenses: For automobile owners, these include payments, insurance, gas, oil, maintenance, depreciation, and auto clubs. For public transportation commuters, this amount includes all bus, train, or subway fees.

Depreciation is the money set aside to repair or replace your vehicle. The minimum amount set aside should be sufficient to keep the car in decent repair and to replace it at least every four to five years. If replacement funds are not available in the budget, the minimum allocation should be maintenance costs.

Annual or semiannual auto insurance payments should be set aside on a monthly basis, thus avoiding the crisis of a neglected expense. Most insurance companies will allow monthly payments on a semiannual renewable policy. However, you need to be aware that there is an additional charge for paying monthly payments.

Although it is important to have a safe, efficient vehicle, it does not have to be the latest or most expensive model.

Many single adults overspend in the area of transportation. The image of a new car, truck, or sports utility vehicle may represent success, eligibility, or security. The fact is that a new vehicle loses a large portion of its resale value as soon as you drive it off the lot. Many singles buy into a leasing plan to "afford" new vehicles they could not afford conventionally. If you have an expensive vehicle, it would be wise to examine your motives for buying it. A good used vehicle is much more practical. As you learn to trust God for your success, eligibility, and security, the easier it will be to let go of the image of a new car.

Category 6

Insurance: This includes all personal insurance, such as health, life, and disability that is not associated with the home or auto. It is common for single adults to be "over-insured" in life insurance and underinsured in disability insurance.

If you do not have immediate family members depending on your income, then you need very little life insurance. A modest policy or the life insurance provided by your employer might be sufficient.

The purpose of life insurance is to provide for those you leave behind who cannot provide for themselves.

However, if you were to face a long-term disability, would you be able to meet your obligations? Most single adults would not. Long-term disability should be a real consideration for single adults without adequate savings.

To decide the correct balance for insurance, a simple test can be used. Can you provide for an unexpected loss yourself? If so, to pay money for insurance is a waste of God's resources. Great emotional appeals can be made for protecting everything from the television to possible termites. At what point do we say enough? That point has been reached when a Christian looks around and finds that trusting God no longer seems necessary for future material needs (Philippians 4:19).

Category 7

Debts: Includes all monthly payments required to meet debt obligations. Home mortgage and automobile payments are not included here.

Many single adults carry a heavy credit debt. It is easy to depend on credit to buffer low-income periods, pay unexpected expenses, or to purchase something on impulse. Many people buy things on credit that they could have saved for. It may have fit

It is not the use of credit that causes the problem; it is the misuse of credit.

into their budgets at the time, but when something unexpected came up they didn't have the funds to handle the emergency, and it added to their debt. It is an escalating problem. It takes concentrated effort to stop the cycle.

This simple rule of thumb will help you determine if you are heading for trouble. If you find that you are unable to pay the full amount owed on credit card debt each month, then it is time to put away the cards. Cut them up if you have to. Because impulse spending is such a major contributor to the problem, we will talk more about impulse spending later.

Category 8

Entertainment and Recreation: This category includes vacation savings, mission trips, singles' activities, camping trips, club dues, sporting equipment, hobby expenses, athletic events, cable TV, and **eating out.**

This category is usually a very expensive area for single adults, and many of them have no idea how much they actually spend on it. Most of these expenses are a matter of necessity to singles, since it may be their only opportunity for socialization. We realize that it is impossible to do everything alone all of the time. It would be very depressing. Going to movies with friends is much more fun than watching TV alone. Although it may be necessary to spend more on activities to meet social needs, there are alternatives to help cut expenses in this category.

Don't subscribe to cable TV movie channels; and take turns with other singles renting videos to watch together.

As mentioned earlier, you can share homemade meals with friends in each other's homes. Participate in an age-appropriate Christian singles group that offers fellowship, spiritual growth, emotional support, and social activities. Make vacation trips more meaningful by serving on mission trips, helping build Habitat homes, or by doing work projects to help other single adults or single parent families in need.

Category 9

Clothing: Figure the average annual amount spent on clothes and divide by 12. If you are not aware of how much you spend on clothes, keep track for three months, add the totals, and divide by three to get the average.

There are two extremes here that many singles fall into. There are those with a sparse, out-of-date wardrobe and those with a closet or two full of clothes they cannot possibly wear. There needs to be a balance. A reasonable amount, about 5 percent of NSI, should be spent to dress appropriately for work and relaxation. Look for good sales or shop consignment stores for quality, classic clothing that won't go out of style by next year.

For those who have two closets full of clothes that are hardly worn, reduce your spending by buying only what you will actually wear, mix and match as much as possible, and avoid fads. Save for that leather coat or special occasion dress. If you haven't worn some things in a year, and they are in great condition and still in style, offer them to someone in need.

Category 10

Savings: Everyone should allocate something for savings. When a surplus above ongoing needs exists, you have the opportunity to transfer savings to investments to meet long-range goals.

A savings account can provide funds for emergencies and is a key element in good planning and financial freedom.

Category 11

Medical Expenses: This includes insurance deductibles and medical bills, eyeglasses, drugs, and dental care not covered by insurance. Use a yearly amount divided by 12 to determine a monthly amount.

After you know how much you need to save per month, you can put the money aside in pretax dollars by participating in your company's salary reduction plan.

Category 12

Miscellaneous: This category is for specific expenses that do not seem to fit anywhere else, such as pocket money, miscellaneous gifts, Christmas presents, toiletries, and haircuts.

It is common for single adults to overspend on gifts for the many social occasions they are invited to, in addition to all the gifts for family members and friends they feel obligated to buy. Often they don't realize that it isn't necessary to spend $40 per gift to attend a social or family occasion. Go in on gift expenses with other friends and family members and share the costs. Draw names with family members so that you only have to buy for one person in the family at Christmas. Shop early and shop sales. If you find a beautiful punchbowl, picture frame, or vase at a good price, buy several and put them away until needed for wedding gifts.

Category 13

Education: It is not uncommon for adults to change occupations two or three times during their working years. Continuing education is a real need. This category is provided to reflect those expenses. *If you are continuing your education, you must reduce all other categories to provide these funds.*

Category 14

Investments: Individuals with a surplus in their budgets will have the opportunity to invest for retirement or other long-term goals, such as purchasing a home, preparing for marriage, caring for elderly parents, or giving larger gifts to Christian organizations. As debt-free status is achieved, more money can be diverted to this category.

Unallocated Income

Category 15

Unallocated Surplus Income: Income from unbudgeted sources (garage sales, gifts, and so on) can be kept in one's checking account and placed in this category. This section can be useful to keep track of surplus income as well as to keep records for tax purposes (see page 52).

Income Versus Expenses

Step One: Compile the expenses under each of the major categories (items 3 through 12) and note this as you total expenses. Then in the space provided, subtract expenses from Net Spendable Income.

Step Two: *If income is greater than expenses,* you need only to control spending to maximize the surplus. Section 6 will help you do this.

Step Three: *If expenses are greater than income,* a detailed analysis will be necessary to correct the situation and restore a proper balance. Proceed to the next section.

Where Are You?

MONTHLY INCOME AND EXPENSES

GROSS INCOME PER MONTH   1,917

Salary	1,917
Interest	
Dividends	
Other (_____)	
Other (_____)	

LESS:

1. **Tithe**   150

2. **Tax** (Est. - Incl. Fed., State, FICA)   402

   NET SPENDABLE INCOME   1,365

3. **Housing**   785

Mortgage (rent)	650
Insurance	10
Taxes	
Electricity	95
Gas	
Water	
Sanitation	
Telephone	30
Maintenance	
Other (_____)	
Other (_____)	

4. **Food**   80

5. **Automobile(s)**   320

Payments	230
Gas and Oil	45
Insurance	40
License/Taxes	5
Maint./Repair/Replace	

6. **Insurance**   15

Life	
Medical	10
Other *DENTAL*	5

7. **Debts**   45

Credit Card	25
Loans and Notes	20
Other (_____)	
Other (_____)	

8. **Enter./Recreation**   150

Eating Out	75
Activities/Trips	40
Vacation	30
Other (_____)	5
Other (_____)	

9. **Clothing**   30

10. **Savings**   25

11. **Medical Expenses**   30

Doctor	25
Dentist	
Drugs	5
Other (_____)	

12. **Miscellaneous**   35

Toiletry, cosmetics	5
Beauty, barber	10
Laundry, cleaning	3
Allowances, lunches	
Subscriptions	
Gifts (incl. Christmas)	10
Cash	7
Cable/Internet	
Other (_____)	
Other (_____)	

13. **Education**

Tuition	
Materials	
Transportation	
Other (_____)	

14. **Investments**

TOTAL EXPENSES   1,515

INCOME VERSUS EXPENSES

Net Spendable Income	1,365
Less Expenses	1,515
	-150

15. **Unallocated Surplus Income** [1]

[1] This category is used when surplus income is received. This would be kept in the checking account to be used within a few weeks; otherwise, it should be transferred to an allocated category.

Figure 2.1

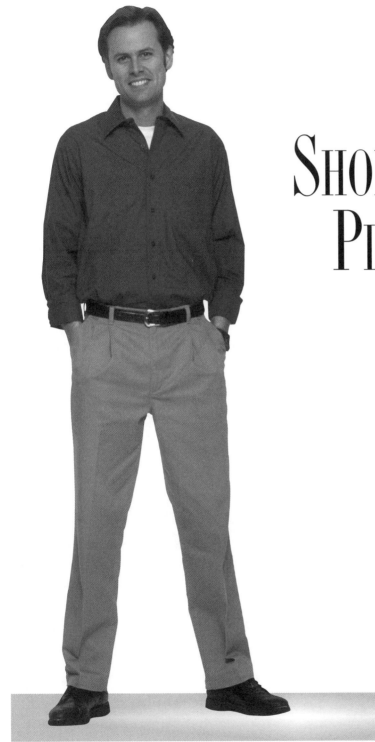

SHORT-RANGE PLANNING

Handling the Variables by Short-Range Planning

What Is Short-Range Planning?

Short-range planning involves budgeting for irregular expenses on a monthly basis. That includes expenses like utility bills, auto maintenance, medical expenses, and clothing. (See Figure 3.1 on page 23.)

Example 1: By averaging utility bills over one year, money can be stored from low-use months to offset the cost of high-use months.

Example 2: Annual or semiannual insurance payments are met by establishing a monthly reserve.

Example 3: Expenditures for clothing and medical or dental bills are other examples for which provision should be made. These items normally are not puchased on a regular basis. Without the needed reserve, paying for these items results in additional debt.

Example 4: A vacation can be planned the same way. Plan what is needed for the coming year's vacation and divide the amount by 12 to determine what must be saved on a monthly basis.

Example 5: Items such as automobiles, appliances, and household goods like furniture, rugs, or draperies wear out or deteriorate over time. Periodic allocations should be made to replace those items as necessary.

Ideally, automobile depreciation and maintenance should be allocated on a monthly basis. That savings would then pay for maintenance, insurance, and replacement of the automobile (assuming the car is kept for five years or 100,000 miles).

Failure to plan for short-range variables and depreciating items results in crisis planning. Control your expenditures; don't let them control you.

A Danger

The tendency in tight budgeting situations is to avoid maintenance and depreciation savings with the excuse that "I just can't afford it." Even if the full amount cannot be set aside, try to save something for those purposes. Depreciation is the same as any other expense. Without money to repair a car, the usual alternative is to replace it—on the time payment plan!

How to Do This

Use the table illustrated in Figure 3.2 (page 24) to determine how much must be allocated to the various categories. For example, if automobile insurance is $420 per year, set aside $35 per month so that the bill can be paid when it is due.

Include those amounts in the proper categories when planning the total budget (use Form 2).

For most people, it is difficult to keep allocated funds available in their checking accounts. The temptation to misspend is too great. To solve this problem, at the end of each month, transfer any allocated money not actually used to your savings account (illustrated in Figure 3.1). The savings ledger will show the various categories for which money is being saved (Form 6). Keep in mind that financial institutions now limit the number of transfers between accounts each month. Therefore, do not transfer any funds that you will need in the near future.

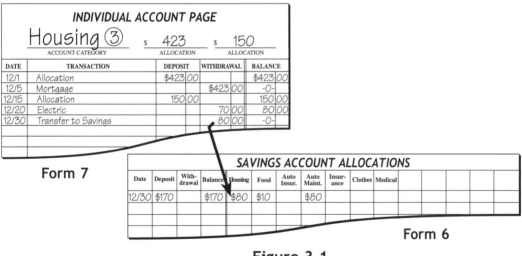

Form 7

Form 6

Figure 3.1

Establish savings account limits. Each account should have a predetermined limit. Once that limit has been reached, no additional savings are necessary.

Example: Let's assume that $600 is the yearly total for your medical expenses. Once the savings for the medical category reaches $600, the needed reserve has been met. Unless greater medical expenses are expected, saving beyond $600 is not necessary. Monthly funds can then be applied elsewhere until a medical expense occurs that reduces the amount in savings.

Remember, the plan is to establish a reserve for variables, depreciating items, maintenance, or special needs, such as fluctuating income. The savings account ledger divides the surplus by budget category.

Be flexible. When starting a budget, it may be necessary to borrow from one account to supplement another. For example, if the car breaks down before a surplus is accumulated in the auto account, it may be necessary to borrow from the clothing or medical accounts to pay for the car repair. However, to continue to do that month after month will defeat the long-range purpose in budgeting.

That purpose is to plan ahead!

	Estimated Cost	Per Month
1. **Vacation**	$ _____ ÷ 12 =	$ _____
2. **Dentist**	$ _____ ÷ 12 =	$ _____
3. **Doctor**	$ _240_ ÷ 12 =	$ _20_
4. **Automobile**	$ _480_ ÷ 12 =	$ _40_
5. **Annual Insurance**	$ _____ ÷ 12 =	$ _____
(Life)	($ _____ ÷ 12 =	$ _____)
(Health)	($ _____ ÷ 12 =	$ _____)
(Auto)	($ _720_ ÷ 12 =	$ _60_)
(Home)	($ _____ ÷ 12 =	$ _____)
6. **Clothing**	$ _600_ ÷ 12 =	$ _50_
7. **Investments**	$ _____ ÷ 12 =	$ _____
8. **Other**	$ _____ ÷ 12 =	$ _____
	$ _____ ÷ 12 =	$ _____

Figure 3.2

LONG-RANGE PLANNING

Long-Range Planning

With ups and downs in the economy and the insecurity of Social Security for those not yet retired, there are plenty of reasons to consider investing. Single adults with a generous income, or those who have lower living expenses, may find that they have more money to invest than those on lower or fixed incomes. There are many people who frugally save and invest the little they have, but others live extravagantly and squander what they could save.

Even though each single adult's need is different, there are 10 common principles or "keys" that can provide a solid foundation for long-range planning. To explore investment options, consult a reputable financial planning expert. Look for someone who does not work on commission for selling products.

Key 1: Formulate clear-cut investment goals.

Retirement. Becoming debt free, including your mortgage, should be your first retirement goal. Once you've achieved that goal, then you should invest in other areas. It is beneficial to remain active after retirement. For many people that means continuing to work—but for fewer hours at a lower wage—and providing more Christian service.

Preservation. If you have inherited a large amount and you want to preserve that money for a particular purpose at a later date, perhaps for a charitable donation, remember that the goal is not to maximize growth but to minimize losses and achieve a reasonable return.

Growth. Some singles may need growth investments to prepare for some long-range plans, such as caring for elderly parents; but others who seek a lot of growth may take big risks, because they're hoping to get rich quick.

Tax Shelters. It is an old wives' tale that paying interest is a good tax shelter. On the other hand, depreciation and investment tax credits can be legitimate tax shelters. Keep in mind that most tax shelters don't eliminate income tax; they only defer it.

Key 2: Avoid personal liability.

Most get-rich-quick schemes, as well as most tax shelters, are available only if you accept personal liability for a large debt. God's Word says to avoid surety, which means never make yourself personally liable for any indebtedness. If you sign a note that says, "If I can't pay the note, the lender has the right to recover the property and sue me for any deficiency," that's surety.

Key 3: Evaluate risks and returns.

There is an important factor in investing called the risk-versus-return ratio. That means, the higher the rate of return, the higher the degree of risk. Before investing in anything riskier than an insured savings account, you need to ask yourself this fundamental question: "Can I really afford to take this risk?" The older you are, the less risk you can take, because it's more difficult to replace the money. If retirement is years away, you may be able to take a higher risk. However, if you need the investment funds to live on right now, then you need the lower risk, regardless of age.

You can lower the risk through education and careful analysis, but you cannot eliminate it.

Key 4: Keep some assets debt free.

If you're using leverage, without surety, to fund some of your investments, it is wise to keep at least 50 percent of all your investment debt free. Leveraging is the use of borrowed money for investing. When you do this, you are expecting that the interest rate charged on the money will be lower than your investment earnings on the money. If at least 50 percent of your investments are debt free, you can never lose everything.

Please note that leveraging is better suited for the experienced investors who know what they're doing. Even then, the risk can be high. Leveraging is not a good idea for the average investor who doesn't have a large surplus.

Key 5: Be patient.

It's important to have your money working for you, but patience will help avoid a great many errors. Remember that greed and speed often work together, so a key to avoiding greed is patience. Most get-rich-quick schemes attract people who don't know what they're doing and who will make investment decisions on the spot. These schemes encourage people to risk money they cannot afford to lose.

Key 6: Diversify.

There's an adage that says, "Don't put all your eggs in one basket." That certainly applies to your investment strategy. Also, split your money into different areas of the economy, such as real estate, gold and silver, stocks and bonds, or certificates of deposit (CDs). The probability is that when one of these areas is down, another will be up. So rather than having to sell one that's down, you could sell one that's up.

Instead of putting all your money into one stock, risking it on how well that one company does, invest in a mutual fund.

Key 7: Long-range trends.

Your investment program should take into account long-range economic trends, especially inflation. When the market is going great, everyone wants to jump in and

> *Remember, with the long-term trends, whatever is going on right now will eventually reverse.*

make a lot of money. Some people who get in will make money, but the vast majority is going to panic during a short-term downturn and lose most or all of the money they have made. People who speculate may wind up losing more than they made, especially if they borrow to invest.

Key 8: Focus on what you own.

Assets don't mean anything. What counts is the amount you own free of liabilities. As mentioned earlier, make it your goal to have at least half your assets totally debt free. If you can't do that right now, make it your number one long-range goal.

Key 9: Know where to sell.

Before you buy, always know where you can sell the investment. The key is very important when you're dealing with so-called exotic investments, such as gemstones, silver, gold, or collectibles. You can do very well buying these items if you know what you're doing. But most people who buy collectibles have no idea of where or how to sell them.

Key 10: Prepare to pass on your investments.

If you will leave an estate to a sibling, niece, nephew, or other family member, that person should be trained in the principles of sound investing. Because most people don't understand investments, they will often liquidate at the wrong time and suffer significant losses. If you will be passing your investments on to a charitable organization, be sure that the details are set up when you establish your portfolio.

For a better understanding of investing, call Crown Financial Ministries about other resources on the subject.

BUDGET
PROBLEMS

BUDGET PROBLEMS

Budget Problem Areas

Beware! Unforeseen problems can wreck your budget. Those include bookkeeping errors, impulse buying, hidden debts, and gifts.

Bookkeeping Errors

An accurately balanced checkbook is a must. Even small errors result in big problems if they are allowed to compound. (A correct procedure is shown in Figure 5.1.)

An inaccurate balance can result in an overdrawn account, as well as in significant bank charges.

Automatic banking systems create additional pitfalls. Automatic payment deductions must be subtracted from the checkbook ledger at the time they are paid by the bank.

Example

An insurance premium is paid by automatic withdrawal on the 15th of each month. Since no statement or notice is received from the insurance company, you must make certain that on the 15th of every month the proper amount is deducted from your home checking account records.

The same would be true for automatic credit card payments or any other automatic withdrawal.

Direct deposits into checking accounts must also be noted in the home ledger at the proper time. **Don't forget** to include bank service charges in the home ledger.

If you withdraw cash from your account at an Automatic Teller Machine (ATM) or process a transaction using a debit card, be sure you write it in your ledger, deduct it immediately, and file the transaction record. Keep the transaction records until you have verified them on your bank statement.

Other Factors in Keeping Good Records

1. Use a ledger type checkbook rather than a stub type. The ledger gives greater visibility and lends itself to fewer errors. Order checks that provide a duplicate copy when a check is written. This eliminates the error of not posting the check.

2. Make certain all checks and transactions are accounted for. All transactions should be entered in the ledger when written. This entry must include the check number if applicable, the amount, the date, and assignee. Tearing checks out of your checkbooks for future use defeats many of the safeguards built into this system. It is wise to write checks only from the checkbook.

CHECKBOOK BALANCE PROCEDURE

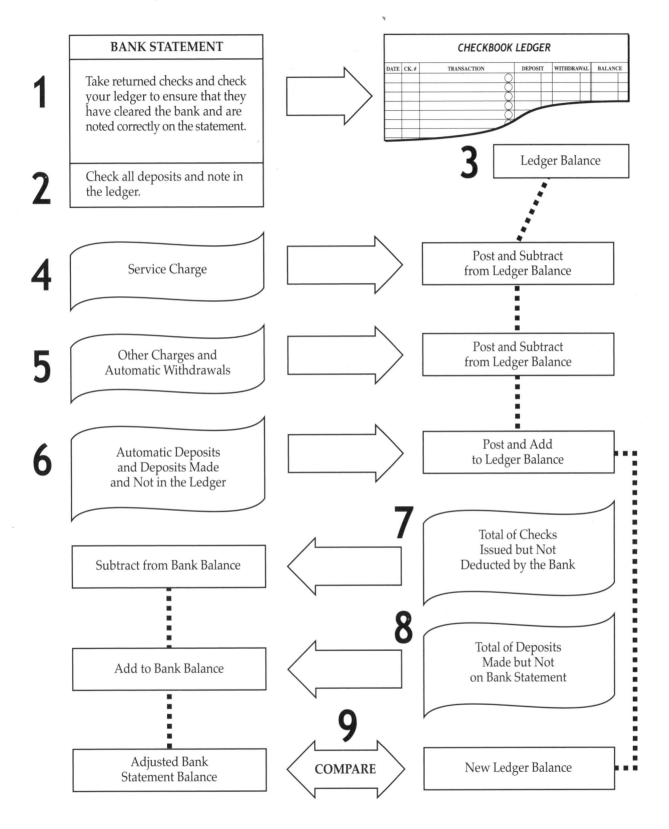

Figure 5.1

3. Maintain a home ledger. If all records are kept in a checkbook ledger, you run the risk of losing it. A home ledger eliminates this possibility and makes record keeping more orderly. Use Form 7a as your checkbook ledger sheet. It is illustrated in Section 8, page 51. The actual form is in the forms section.

4. Balance the account every month—to the penny. Never allow the home ledger and bank statement to disagree in balance. The two most common errors are arithmetic errors (addition or subtraction) and transposition errors (writing in the wrong amount). Use a calculator and balance the account **to the penny.**

Hidden Debts

A common error is to overlook nonmonthly debts, such as doctor bills, family loans, and bank notes. Thus, when payments come due, there is no budget allocation for them.

To avoid surprises, establish and maintain a list of debts in total. The list must be reviewed and revised on a periodic basis, and the budget must anticipate necessary payments.

Begin with a goal of eliminating the smallest debt first.

The list should reflect progress made on debt payments and can serve as a "payoff goal" sheet. Then use the funds allocated for the first debt to double your payment on the next debt—and so on until all debts are eliminated.

Form 8 in the forms section (page 55) is provided to list all outstanding debts. A copy is shown in Figure 5.2 on page 34. Note that space is provided for the name and number of the person to contact in the event of a problem.

Impulse Buying

Impulse items are unnecessary purchases made on the spur of the moment.

These purchases are usually rationalized by, "It was on sale," "I was planning to buy it anyway," "I've always wanted one," "I just couldn't resist it," "or "I owe it to myself." Often they are made with a credit card because the cash isn't available. The net result is a little-used item and an unnecessary debt.

Impulse purchases are not restricted to small items. They range from homes, cars, and trips to unscheduled luncheons. Cost is not the issue; necessity is. Every purchase should be considered in light of the budget.

Discipline is the key to controlling impulse buying. If necessary, resort to the self-imposed discipline of the Impulse List in Figure 5.2 on page 34.

Establish the discipline that before buying on impulse you will list the item on the impulse sheet, along with the date and the cost. Then wait 30 days before purchasing the item. During that time compare the price of the item in at least two additional places.

If you feel you still need the item after 30 days and the money is available, then buy it. You will eliminate most impulse items by this discipline.

Accountability

As mentioned earlier, single adults are alone when making financial decisions. They are not accountable to anyone, except for their creditors. This can be a blessing and a curse. You have more liberty to spend your money the way you want to, but you also have no one to help you balance your decisions. If you're a spender, no one tells you that you're spending too much. If you're a saver, no one tells you when you need to give. If you're a giver, no one tells you when to save.

Even after you develop a budget using this workbook, it is very important for you, as a single adult, to develop an accountability relationship with someone you trust. This can be a prayer partner, a married couple, or another single adult whom you respect and who makes sound financial decisions.

It is very important for you, as a single adult, to develop an accountability relationship with someone you trust.

This person should be your sounding board, prayer partner, and someone who brings balance to your personality and spending style. If no one like that is available to you, then call or write to Crown Financial Ministries for a budget counselor in your area.

Gifts

As mentioned, a major budget-buster for most people is overspending on gifts. Tradition dictates a gift for nearly every occasion. Unfortunately, the net result is often a gift someone doesn't want, purchased with money that was needed for something else.

Many times the cost is increased because the gift is selected at the last moment. If gifts are a part of normal spending, budget for them and buy ahead—reasonably.

To bring the cost of gifts under control, consider the following.

1. Keep an event calendar for the year and budget ahead.

2. Determine not to buy any gifts on credit (especially Christmas gifts).

3. Draw family names for selected gifts rather than giving to everyone.

4. Go in with friends or family members to purchase a gift.

LIST OF DEBTS
as of _____

TO WHOM OWED	CONTACT NAME / PHONE NUMBER	PAY OFF	PAYMENTS LEFT	MONTHLY PAYMENT	DUE DATE

IMPULSE LIST

DATE	IMPULSE ITEM	1	2	3

Figure 5.2

THE
GUIDELINE
BUDGET

What Is a Guideline Budget?

The guideline budget is the amount you have to spend divided into percentages to help determine the proper balance for each category of the budget.

The primary use of the guideline is to indicate problem areas. The percentages are based on the average incomes of single males or females living alone or with a roommate. The percentages may change according to your situation and needs. In the lower income levels, basic needs will dominate the income distribution. Percentage guidelines are shown in Figure 6.1.

Purpose of a Guideline

The guideline is developed to determine a standard against which to compare present spending patterns. It will serve as a basis for determining areas of overspending that are creating the greatest problems. Additionally, it helps determine where adjustments need to be made. If you are overspending, the percentage guidelines can be used as a goal for budgeting. Although the percentages are guides only, and not absolutes, they do help establish upper levels of spending.

For instance, if you're spending 40 percent or more of your Net Spendable Income on Housing, you may have difficulty balancing your budget. You may have a little more flexibility than families with children, who spend more on Housing or Automobiles.

Guideline Percentages

The Net Spendable Income is used to calculate the ideal spending for each budget category. Net Spendable Income is determined by subtracting your tithe and taxes from your gross income. If taxes are known, then actual amounts can be used. In the example shown in Figure 6.2 on page 38, Net Spendable Income is $1,322 per month. Thus, for Housing, 40 percent of NSI equals $529 per month. According to this guideline, no more than $529 should be spent for Housing. That includes rent or home payment, taxes, insurance, utilities, and upkeep.

Example

If 45 percent of the NSI is used for Housing, the percentage for Food and Transportation must be reduced.

Note that in some categories there are many variables, such as utilities and taxes. To accommodate this, you must adjust percentages within ranges under Housing, Food, and Transportation. However, those three together should never exceed 65 percent of your NSI.

PERCENTAGE GUIDE FOR INDIVIDUAL INCOME

(unmarried adults)

	FEMALE LIVING ALINE	FEMALE WITH ROOMMATE	MALE LIVING ALINE	MALE WITH ROOMMATE
Gross Income	$23,000	$23,000	$32,000	$32,000
1. Tithe	10%	10%	10%	10%
2. Tax	21%	21%	24%	24%
Net Spendable Income (per month)	$1,322	$1,322	$1,760	$1,760
3. Housing	40%	25%	38%	22%
4. Food	6%	6%	6%	6%
5. Auto	15%	20%	15%	15%
6. Insurance	4%	4%	4%	4%
7. Debts	5%	5%	5%	5%
8. Enter./Recreation	8%	10%	7%	10%
9. Clothing	5%	5%	5%	5%
10. Savings	7%	15%	6%	19%
11. Medical	5%	5%	7%	7%
12. Miscellaneous	5%	5%	7%	7%
13. Education[1]	3%	10%	7%	10%
14. Investments[2]	5%	5%	8%	10%
15. Unallocated Surplus Income[3]	—	—	—	—

1. This category is added as a guide only. If you have this expense, the percentage shown must be deducted from other budget categories.

2. This category is used for long-term investment planning, such as caring for elderly parents or retirement.

3. This category is used when surplus income is received. This would be kept in the checking account to be used within a few weeks; otherwise, it should be transferred to an allocated category.

Figure 6.1

37

The next step? Budget Analysis.

BUDGET PERCENTAGE GUIDELINES

Salary for guideline = $_____23,000_____/year[1]

Gross Income Per Month $_____1,917_____

1. Tithe	(10 % of Gross)	(1,917)	= $	192
2. Tax	(21 % of Gross)	(1,917)	= $	403

Net Spendable Income $_____1,322_____

3. Housing	(40 % of Net)	(1,322)	= $	529
4. Food	(6 % of Net)	(1,322)	= $	79
5. Auto	(15 % of Net)	(1,322)	= $	198
6. Insurance	(4 % of Net)	(1,322)	= $	53
7. Debts	(5 % of Net)	(1,322)	= $	66
8. Enter./Rec.	(8 % of Net)	(1,322)	= $	106
9. Clothing	(5 % of Net)	(1,322)	= $	66
10. Savings	(7 % of Net)	(1,322)	= $	93
11. Medical	(5 % of Net)	(1,322)	= $	66
12. Miscellaneous	(5 % of Net)	(1,322)	= $	66
13. Education	(___ % of Net)	(_____)	= $	
14. Investments	(___ % of Net)	(_____)	= $	

Total (Cannot exceed Net Spendable Income) $_____1,322_____

15. Unallocated Surplus Income   (___N/A___) = $ _____

1. Refer to page 37 for percentage guidelines.

Figure 6.2

BUDGET ANALYSIS

BUDGET ANALYSIS

After determining the present spending level (where you are), and reviewing the guideline percentages (where you should be), the task becomes one of developing a new budget that handles the areas of overspending. Keep in mind that the total expenditures must not exceed the Net Spendable Income. If you have more spendable income than expenses, you need to control spending to maximize your surplus.

The Budget Analysis page (Figure 7.1) provides space for summarizing both actual expenses and guideline expenses on one sheet—for working convenience. The total amounts of each category from the monthly Income and Expense sheet (Figure 2.1, page 19) and from the Percentage Guide for Individual Income (Figure 6.1, page 37) should be transferred to the appropriate columns on the Budget Analysis page.

Step One: Compare

The **Existing Budget** and **Guideline** columns should be compared. Note the difference, plus or minus, in the Difference column. A negative notation indicates a deficit; a positive notation indicates a surplus. The budget shown is the actual spending of a typical single adult.

Step Two: Analyze

After comparing the **Existing** and **Guideline** columns, decisions must be made about overspending. It may be possible to reduce some areas to compensate for overspending in others. For example, if Housing expenditures are more than 38 percent, it may be necessary to sacrifice in areas like Entertainment and Recreation, Miscellaneous, and Transportation. If debts exceed 5 percent, then the problems are compounded.

Note the flexibility gained if you are not in debt. That 5 percent is available for use elsewhere in the budget.

Ultimately, the decision becomes one of where and how to cut back.

It is not necessary that your new budget fit the guideline budget. It is necessary that your new budget does not exceed your Net Spendable Income.

Step Three: Decide

Once the total picture is reviewed, it is necessary to decide where adjustments must be made and spending reduced. You may have to consider a change in Housing, Transportation, or Insurance.

The **minimum** objective of any budget should be to meet your needs without creating any further debt.

BUDGET ANALYSIS

Per Year $ 23,000   Net Spendable Income
Per Month $ 1,917   Per Month $ 1,322

MONTHLY PAYMENT CATEGORY	EXISTING BUDGET	MONTHLY GUIDELINE BUDGET	DIFFERENCE + OR -	NEW MONTHLY BUDGET
1. Tithe	150	192	+ 42	192
2. Tax	403	403	0	403
Net Spendable Income (per month)	$ 1,364	$ 1,322	$ - 42	$ 1,322
3. Housing	785	529	- 265	435
4. Food	80	79	- 1	80
5. Auto	320	198	- 122	225
6. Insurance	15	53	+ 38	30
7. Debts	45	66	+ 21	100
8. Enter./Recreation	150	106	- 44	110
9. Clothing	30	66	+ 36	50
10. Savings	25	93	+ 68	100
11. Medical	30	66	+ 36	50
12. Miscellaneous	35	66	+ 31	50
13. Education	–			
14. Investments	–			92
Totals (Items 3-14)	$ 1,515	$ 1,322		$ 1,322

15. Unallocated Surplus Income				

Figure 7.1

If you failed the credit test and cannot pay your credit cards off each month, or you have accumulated long-term debt, it may be necessary to negotiate with creditors to pay smaller amounts per month. It's better to establish an amount you can pay than to promise an amount you cannot pay. If you are unable to negotiate with creditors on your own to create a repayment plan, you may want to contact Consumer Credit Counseling Service of Atlanta. They are very familiar with Crown Financial Ministries and offer telephone counseling. They can be reached by calling (888) 771-HOPE (4673).

Beware of consolidation loans, refinancing, and more borrowing. They are not the solutions; they are merely symptom treatments.

The solution comes from discipline, sacrifice, and trusting God to supply needs.

After a new budget has been determined, you are ready to proceed to the allocation and control system.

How the adjustments were made.

1. Tithe

The tithe was increased to 10 percent of gross income.

2. Taxes

Taxes remained the same since there were no deductibles that warranted an itemized return.

3. Housing

Housing was reduced to $435 per month because this person decided to take in a roommate for a while to save money. The roommate will pay $350 per month.

4. Food

The food budget needed no adjustments, because it fit within the guideline.

5. Auto/Transportation

This person was paying $230 a month for a late model car. The car was sold and a less expensive model was purchased for $125 per month. With gas, oil, maintenance, and insurance, the total is now $225 per month.

6. Insurance

Disability insurance was added since there was no appreciable savings to fall back on in time of need.

7. Debts

This was increased to $100 per month to eliminate existing debt. Credit cards were canceled. This shows commitment and paves the way for totally paying off these debts in future months.

8. Enter./Recreation

This category was reduced to $110 per month, at least until debts are paid. Better methods of socializing were suggested to cut expenses, which still remained slightly higher than the guideline. If there is a need to cut further in this area, be careful not to eliminate it entirely; just cut it back.

9. Clothing

This category was under-budgeted, so $20 per month was added.

10. Savings

This was increased to $100 per month. As a single adult, this person needed to develop some funds to fall back on when emergencies arise or the unexpected happens, such as an unpaid leave from work.

11. Medical

This was another under-allocation. It was increased to $50 per month.

12. Miscellaneous

This category was increased to $50 per month.

13. Education

No attempt was made to budget for this category at this time. If funds are needed in the future, the other categories must be adjusted accordingly.

14. Investments

Once an adequate emergency fund is established, additional income may be invested for long-term goals. This person's goal is to live alone by purchasing a home at some future date.

15. Unallocated Surplus Income

If there is a surplus income at any time, it will be placed in this category for future use as needed, donated as gifts to ministries, or directed toward debt reduction or investments.

THE CONTROL SYSTEM

THE CONTROL SYSTEM

Accounting - Allocation - Control

A budget that is not used is a waste of time and effort. The most common reason a budget is discarded is because it's too complicated.

The system described in this workbook is the simplest, yet most complete, possible.

Keep It Simple

The Goal

Establish a level of spending for each category so that more money coming in does not mean more money to spend and so that you know where you are with respect to that level at all times.

This budget system is analogous to the old envelope system. In the past, many employers paid earnings in cash. To control spending, people established an effective system by dividing the available money into the various budget categories (Housing, Food, Clothes, and so on) and holding it in individual envelopes.

As a need or payment came due, money was withdrawn from the appropriate envelope and spent.

The system was simple and, when used properly, quite effective for controlling spending. The rule was simple: When an envelope was empty, there could be no more spending for that category. Money could be taken from another envelope, but a decision had to be made—immediately.

Since most people today are paid by check, and since holding cash in the home is not always advisable, a different allocation system is necessary.

It is important to know how much should be spent, how much is being spent, and how much is left to spend in each budget category. To accomplish this, account control pages have been substituted for envelopes. All the money is deposited into a checking account, and account control pages are used to accomplish what the envelopes once accomplished. How much to put into

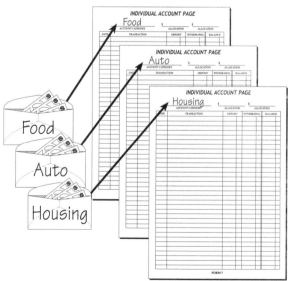

each account (or envelope) from monies received during the month is determined from the Income Allocation sheet.

Use of the Income Allocation Page (Form 5)

The purpose of the Income Allocation page is to divide Net Spendable Income among the various budget categories. It is simply a predetermined plan of how each paycheck or income source is going to be spent.

Once you have determined from the Budget Analysis (page 41) how much can be spent in each category per month, write it in the **Monthly Allocation** column.

Next, divide the monthly allocation for each category (Housing, Food, and so forth) by pay period.

Example

(For income received twice each month) Note that the mortgage payment is made on the 29th of the month so the allocation must be divided in a manner to make sure that adequate funds are available at the time the payment is due. Utility and maintenance payments would have to be made from another pay period.

	Allocation	Pay period	
HOUSING	$573	$423	$150
FOOD	$200	$100	$100
AUTO	$260	$160	$160
INSURANCE	$39	$14	$25

It is not mandatory that checks be divided evenly. The important thing is that when a payment is due the money is available. Therefore, some reserve funds from middle-of-the-month pay periods must be held to meet obligations that come due at the first of the month. Failure to do this is a common source of budget problems.

Use of the Individual Account Pages (Form 7)

A separate account page is used for each budget category (Housing, Food, Auto/Transportation, and so on), just as each had its own envelope under the cash system.

At the top of the page, the proper account title is entered, such as Housing or Food,

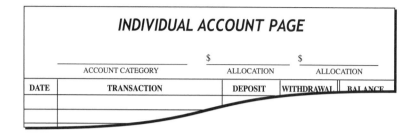

INDIVIDUAL ACCOUNT PAGE				
ACCOUNT CATEGORY	$ ALLOCATION		$ ALLOCATION	
DATE	TRANSACTION	DEPOSIT	WITHDRAWAL	BALANCE

together with the monthly allocation. Each account sheet has two blanks ($_____). These are used to write in your allocation for a twice-monthly pay period. If you are paid more frequently, just add more blanks ($_____).

The purpose of the account sheet is to document **all** transactions for the month. The pay period allowance or allocation is shown as a deposit, and each time money is spent it is shown as a withdrawal.

If funds are left at the end of the month, the account page is zeroed by transferring the money to the savings account. If an account runs short, then it may be necessary to transfer money from savings to the appropriate account. When an account is out of money, a decision must be made concerning how it is going to be treated. (See Figure 8.1.)

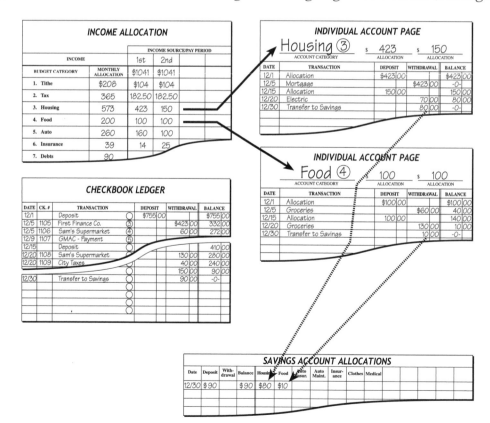

Figure 8.1

How to Use the Budget System

A good budget system should be kept as simple as possible while still accomplishing its goal: **to indicate whether you spend more than you allocated for each month.** Remember that this system is analogous to using envelopes. If a specific amount of money is placed in envelopes each month, you will know at a glance whether or not your budget balances. Obviously with some nonmonthly expenses to be budgeted, the ledger system has to be a little more complicated, but don't overcomplicate it.

To help you better understand how to use the budget system, we will take one category (Housing) through a typical month's transactions.

INCOME ALLOCATION

		INCOME SOURCE/PAY PERIOD			
INCOME		1st	2nd		
BUDGET CATEGORY	MONTHLY ALLOCATION	$1041	$1041		
1. Tithe	$208	$104	$104		
2. Tax	365	182.50	182.50		
3. Housing	573	423	150		
4. Food	200	100	100		
5. Auto	260	160	100		
6. Insurance	39	14	25		
7. Debts	90				

INDIVIDUAL ACCOUNT PAGE

Housing ③ $ 423 $ 150
ACCOUNT CATEGORY   ALLOCATION   ALLOCATION

DATE	TRANSACTION	DEPOSIT	WITHDRAWAL	BALANCE
12/1	Allocation	$423 00		$423 00
12/5	Mortgage		$423 00	-0-
12/15	Allocation	150 00		150 00
12/20	Electric		70 00	80 00
12/30	Transfer to Savings		80 00	-0-

Figure 8.2

Figure 8.2 shows a typical budget in which the gross income of $2,083 per month is received in two pay periods of $1,041 each.

Pay Allocation—The two checks have been divided as evenly as possible among the necessary categories. For example, the tithe is paid each pay period (remember, it is based on gross income). The housing allocation of $573 is divided: $423 in the first pay period, $150 in the second.

Housing Allocation—On the first pay period, a deposit of $423 is noted on the account page. On the 5th of the month, the mortgage is paid and noted as a withdrawal, leaving a balance of zero.

Each transaction is noted similarly until, at the end of the month, a balance of $80 is left. This balance is then transferred to Savings, as are month-end balances from the other account pages (Food, Savings, and so on). Hence, each account starts at zero the next month.

Many people prefer to leave the surplus funds from each category in their checking accounts rather than transfer them to savings accounts, since many institutions now

> **Note**
>
> *In many cases, the Housing account may have to carry a surplus forward to make the mortgage payment, if it comes due on the 1st of the month.*

limit the number of transactions between accounts. This is fine, if you can discipline yourself not to spend the money just because it's easily accessible. Often the total cash reserves in checking are enough to qualify for free checking privileges, which more than off-set any loss of interest in a savings account.

Use of the Checkbook Ledger

To simplify your bookkeeping, I recommend using one of the Individual Account pages (Form 7) as a checkbook ledger. If you also use a checkbook that gives you a duplicate copy of each check written, it will reduce the number of steps in the book-keeping process.

Note that the Checkbook Ledger (Form 7a) is just a slightly modified Form 7. Each deposit and withdrawal is recorded, and the outstanding balance is shown. At the end of each month, the ledger is balanced against the bank statement. Also, the total balance in the ledger is then compared to the balance on the budget account sheets.

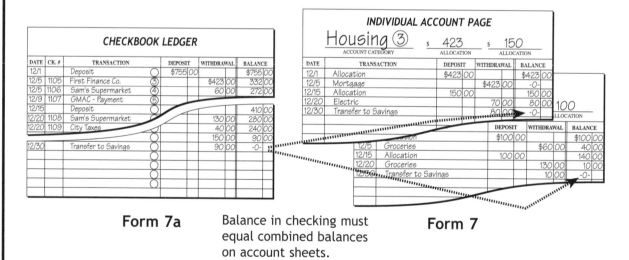

Form 7a

Balance in checking must equal combined balances on account sheets.

Form 7

If there are additional deposits or withdrawals from the bank statement recorded in the Checkbook Ledger, these must also be posted in the appropriate Individual Account pages. For example, a service charge from the bank would be posted as an expense in the Checkbook Ledger and as a Miscellaneous expense in Category 12 of the budget.

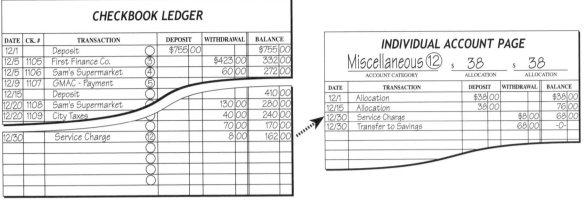

Form 7a　　　　　　　　　　　**Form 7**

Note that the circle (O) on Form 7a is used to indicate the category to which the check has been allocated in the budget. This is filled in **only** after the check has been recorded in the proper budget category.

Checking Account Notation

The common practice with many budgeters is to write the checks, record (post) the checks in the Ledger (Figure 8.3), and then record the transactions in the Individual Account pages at a later time. To ensure that all checks are recorded in the Account sheets, a notation of the category number should be made for each entry in the Checkbook Ledger in the appropriate block.

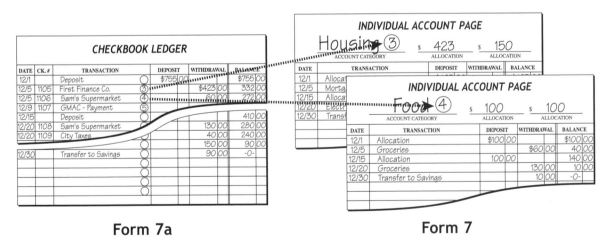

Form 7a　　　　　　　　　　　**Form 7**

Figure 8.3

Keep in mind that the goal of the system is to establish a level of spending for each category and to know where you are with respect to that level.

The account pages ("envelopes") keep track of money in the checking account. The Savings Account Allocation page keeps track of money in the Savings account. However, you may want to use a Savings Account page (or envelope) within the checking account to minimize transfers to and from the savings account.

Remember, the plan is to know what each dollar in the checking account is for and what each dollar in the savings account is for. When you spend money, you need to know which money is spent (Clothes money, Food money, Medical money).

Use of Category 15 —
Surplus Income (Larry's solution)

I have found in using the budget system myself that sometimes I had extra money available above what I had budgeted. I could have simply transferred it to my Savings category and often did so, if the money was to be used several months later. But if the money was going to be used within a few weeks, I wanted to leave it in the checking account. Since I didn't want it allocated to any of the regular monthly categories, I created a 15th category just to hold these surplus funds. This allowed me to keep each of the other categories constant each month. You may find this system helpful if you periodically have extra income that is unallocated. It also serves as a good record of income for tax purposes.

Discipline

In order to provide the necessary control, you must discipline yourself to spend money based on the bottom line of the applicable envelope and not based on the bottom line of the checkbook.

Potential Problem Areas

Cash Withdrawals—Many times miscellaneous expenditures for car expenses, gas, and other items are made with personal cash. In establishing a budget, it is important to develop some rules for self-discipline.

1. Separate personal cash into categories identical to the account pages. Use envelopes if necessary, but avoid spending gas money for lunches and grocery money for entertainment.

2. When all the money has been spent from a category (Entertainment, Miscellaneous, or whatever) **stop spending.**

3. Don't write checks for amounts in excess of actual purchases to get cash. Write another check and note it as "cash, personal."

Category Mixing—Don't try to make the record keeping more complicated than necessary. This system should require no more than 30 minutes per week to maintain. If you choose to develop more detailed breakdowns of expenses and savings, wait until the budget has been in use at least six months.

Automatic Overdrafts

Many banks offer an automatic overdraft protection service. Thus, if you write a check in excess of what you have in your account, the bank will still honor it. On the surface this looks like a helpful service. However, it has been my experience that the overdraft protection tends to create a complacent attitude about balancing the account and encourages overdrafting. Since these charges are accrued to a credit account, you will have to pay interest on your overdrafts. I recommend that these services be avoided until the budgeting routine is well established. Hopefully, by then they will be unnecessary.

Budgeting on a Variable Income

One of the most difficult problems in budgeting is how to allocate monthly spending when your income fluctuates, as it often does on commission sales or if you are self-employed. The normal tendency is to spend the money as it comes in. This works great during the higher-income months but usually causes havoc during the lower-income months.

Two suggestions will help anyone living on a fluctuating income: First, always separate any business-related expenses, such as car maintenance, meals, and living accommodations from your normal household expenses.

I recommend a separate checking account for business expenses and separate credit cards, if needed.

Second, you need to estimate what your (low) average income for one year will be and generate your monthly budget based on the **average income per month.** As the funds come in, they need to be deposited into a special savings account and a salary drawn from the account. The effect is to ration the income over the year in relatively equal amounts that can be budgeted.

Remember, if you are self-employed, you'll need to budget for payroll taxes on a quarterly basis. Failure to do this will result in a rather unpleasant visit with representatives of the Internal Revenue Service.

If you are beginning your budget during one of the lower income months, you may have to delay funding some of the variable expenses, such as clothing, vacations, dental, or the like. These can be funded later when the income allows.

What If You Are Paid Every Two Weeks?

If you happen to be paid every two weeks rather than twice monthly, you will have two extra paychecks a year. I recommend using these paychecks to fund some of the nonmonthly expenses, such as car repair, vacation, and clothing. The same would be true of tax refunds, bonuses, and gifts.

The Results

Although many people struggle with budgeting, we have received hundreds of testimonies about the results. Many people who were facing a great deal of indebtedness began taking these principles seriously and began budgeting. Now they write us with stories of paying off those debts before expected. Laying their finances out on paper gave them perspective and something specific to submit to God. When financial freedom comes, it is well worth the effort.

BEGIN NOW: FORMS

MONTHLY INCOME AND EXPENSES

GROSS INCOME PER MONTH _____

    Salary _____

    Interest _____

    Dividends _____

    Other (_____) _____

    Other (_____) _____

LESS:

1. **Tithe** _____

2. **Tax** (Est. - Incl. Fed., State, FICA) _____

    NET SPENDABLE INCOME _____

3. **Housing** _____

    Mortgage (rent) _____

    Insurance _____

    Taxes _____

    Electricity _____

    Gas _____

    Water _____

    Sanitation _____

    Telephone _____

    Maintenance _____

    Other (_____) _____

    Other (_____) _____

4. **Food** _____

5. **Automobile(s)** _____

    Payments _____

    Gas and Oil _____

    Insurance _____

    License/Taxes _____

    Maint./Repair/Replace _____

6. **Insurance** _____

    Life _____

    Medical _____

    Other _____

7. **Debts** _____

    Credit Card _____

    Loans and Notes _____

    Other (_____) _____

    Other (_____) _____

8. **Enter./Recreation** _____

    Eating Out _____

    Activities/Trips _____

    Vacation _____

    Other (_____) _____

    Other (_____) _____

9. **Clothing** _____

10. **Savings** _____

11. **Medical Expenses** _____

    Doctor _____

    Dentist _____

    Drugs _____

    Other (_____) _____

12. **Miscellaneous** _____

    Toiletry, cosmetics _____

    Beauty, barber _____

    Laundry, cleaning _____

    Allowances, lunches _____

    Subscriptions _____

    Gifts (incl. Christmas) _____

    Cash _____

    Cable/Internet _____

    Other (_____) _____

    Other (_____) _____

13. **Education** _____

    Tuition _____

    Materials _____

    Transportation _____

    Other (_____) _____

14. **Investments** _____

    TOTAL EXPENSES _____

INCOME VERSUS EXPENSES

    Net Spendable Income _____

    Less Expenses _____

15. **Unallocated Surplus Income** [1] _____

[1] This category is used when surplus income is received. This would be kept in the checking account to be used within a few weeks; otherwise, it should be transferred to an allocated category.

FORM 1

MONTHLY INCOME AND EXPENSES

GROSS INCOME PER MONTH _____

    Salary _____

    Interest _____

    Dividends _____

    Other (_____) _____

    Other (_____) _____

LESS:

1. **Tithe** _____

2. **Tax** (Est. - Incl. Fed., State, FICA) _____

NET SPENDABLE INCOME _____

3. **Housing** _____
   - Mortgage (rent) _____
   - Insurance _____
   - Taxes _____
   - Electricity _____
   - Gas _____
   - Water _____
   - Sanitation _____
   - Telephone _____
   - Maintenance _____
   - Other (_____) _____
   - Other (_____) _____

4. **Food** _____

5. **Automobile(s)** _____
   - Payments _____
   - Gas and Oil _____
   - Insurance _____
   - License/Taxes _____
   - Maint./Repair/Replace _____

6. **Insurance** _____
   - Life _____
   - Medical _____
   - Other _____

7. **Debts** _____
   - Credit Card _____
   - Loans and Notes _____
   - Other (_____) _____
   - Other (_____) _____

8. **Enter./Recreation** _____
   - Eating Out _____
   - Activities/Trips _____
   - Vacation _____
   - Other (_____) _____
   - Other (_____) _____

9. **Clothing** _____

10. **Savings** _____

11. **Medical Expenses** _____
    - Doctor _____
    - Dentist _____
    - Drugs _____
    - Other (_____) _____

12. **Miscellaneous** _____
    - Toiletry, cosmetics _____
    - Beauty, barber _____
    - Laundry, cleaning _____
    - Allowances, lunches _____
    - Subscriptions _____
    - Gifts (incl. Christmas) _____
    - Cash _____
    - Cable/Internet _____
    - Other (_____) _____
    - Other (_____) _____

13. **Education** _____
    - Tuition _____
    - Materials _____
    - Transportation _____
    - Other (_____) _____

14. **Investments** _____

TOTAL EXPENSES _____

INCOME VERSUS EXPENSES

    Net Spendable Income _____

    Less Expenses _____

15. **Unallocated Surplus Income** [1] _____

[1] This category is used when surplus income is received. This would be kept in the checking account to be used within a few weeks; otherwise, it should be transferred to an allocated category.

FORM 1

MONTHLY INCOME AND EXPENSES

GROSS INCOME PER MONTH _____

    Salary _____

    Interest _____

    Dividends _____

    Other (_____) _____

    Other (_____) _____

LESS:

1. **Tithe** _____

2. **Tax** (Est. - Incl. Fed., State, FICA) _____

    NET SPENDABLE INCOME _____

3. **Housing** _____

    Mortgage (rent) _____

    Insurance _____

    Taxes _____

    Electricity _____

    Gas _____

    Water _____

    Sanitation _____

    Telephone _____

    Maintenance _____

    Other (_____) _____

    Other (_____) _____

4. **Food** _____

5. **Automobile(s)** _____

    Payments _____

    Gas and Oil _____

    Insurance _____

    License/Taxes _____

    Maint./Repair/Replace _____

6. **Insurance** _____

    Life _____

    Medical _____

    Other _____

7. **Debts** _____

    Credit Card _____

    Loans and Notes _____

    Other (_____) _____

    Other (_____) _____

8. **Enter./Recreation** _____

    Eating Out _____

    Activities/Trips _____

    Vacation _____

    Other (_____) _____

    Other (_____) _____

9. **Clothing** _____

10. **Savings** _____

11. **Medical Expenses** _____

    Doctor _____

    Dentist _____

    Drugs _____

    Other (_____) _____

12. **Miscellaneous** _____

    Toiletry, cosmetics _____

    Beauty, barber _____

    Laundry, cleaning _____

    Allowances, lunches _____

    Subscriptions _____

    Gifts (incl. Christmas) _____

    Cash _____

    Cable/Internet _____

    Other (_____) _____

    Other (_____) _____

13. **Education** _____

    Tuition _____

    Materials _____

    Transportation _____

    Other (_____) _____

14. **Investments** _____

    TOTAL EXPENSES _____

INCOME VERSUS EXPENSES

    Net Spendable Income _____

    Less Expenses _____

15. **Unallocated Surplus Income** [1] _____

[1] This category is used when surplus income is received. This would be kept in the checking account to be used within a few weeks; otherwise, it should be transferred to an allocated category.

FORM 1

MONTHLY INCOME AND EXPENSES

GROSS INCOME PER MONTH _____

    Salary _____

    Interest _____

    Dividends _____

    Other (_____) _____

    Other (_____) _____

LESS:

1. **Tithe** _____

2. **Tax** (Est. - Incl. Fed., State, FICA) _____

NET SPENDABLE INCOME _____

3. **Housing** _____

    Mortgage (rent) _____

    Insurance _____

    Taxes _____

    Electricity _____

    Gas _____

    Water _____

    Sanitation _____

    Telephone _____

    Maintenance _____

    Other (_____) _____

    Other (_____) _____

4. **Food** _____

5. **Automobile(s)** _____

    Payments _____

    Gas and Oil _____

    Insurance _____

    License/Taxes _____

    Maint./Repair/Replace _____

6. **Insurance** _____

    Life _____

    Medical _____

    Other _____

7. **Debts** _____

    Credit Card _____

    Loans and Notes _____

    Other (_____) _____

    Other (_____) _____

8. **Enter./Recreation** _____

    Eating Out _____

    Activities/Trips _____

    Vacation _____

    Other (_____) _____

    Other (_____) _____

9. **Clothing** _____

10. **Savings** _____

11. **Medical Expenses** _____

    Doctor _____

    Dentist _____

    Drugs _____

    Other (_____) _____

12. **Miscellaneous** _____

    Toiletry, cosmetics _____

    Beauty, barber _____

    Laundry, cleaning _____

    Allowances, lunches _____

    Subscriptions _____

    Gifts (incl. Christmas) _____

    Cash _____

    Cable/Internet _____

    Other (_____) _____

    Other (_____) _____

13. **Education** _____

    Tuition _____

    Materials _____

    Transportation _____

    Other (_____) _____

14. **Investments** _____

TOTAL EXPENSES _____

INCOME VERSUS EXPENSES

    Net Spendable Income _____

    Less Expenses _____

15. **Unallocated Surplus Income** [1] _____

[1] This category is used when surplus income is received. This would be kept in the checking account to be used within a few weeks; otherwise, it should be transferred to an allocated category.

FORM 1

VARIABLE EXPENSE PLANNING

Plan for those expenses that are not paid on a regular monthly basis by estimating the yearly cost and determining the monthly amount needed to be set aside for that expense. A helpful formula is to allow the previous year's expense and add 5 percent.

	Estimated Cost		Per Month
1. Vacation	$ _____	÷ 12 =	$ _____
2. Dentist	$ _____	÷ 12 =	$ _____
3. Doctor	$ _____	÷ 12 =	$ _____
4. Automobile	$ _____	÷ 12 =	$ _____
5. Annual Insurance	$ _____	÷ 12 =	$ _____
(Life)	($ _____	÷ 12 =	$ _____)
(Health)	($ _____	÷ 12 =	$ _____)
(Auto)	($ _____	÷ 12 =	$ _____)
(Home)	($ _____	÷ 12 =	$ _____)
6. Clothing	$ _____	÷ 12 =	$ _____
7. Investments	$ _____	÷ 12 =	$ _____
8. Other	$ _____	÷ 12 =	$ _____
	$ _____	÷ 12 =	$ _____

FORM 2

VARIABLE EXPENSE PLANNING

Plan for those expenses that are not paid on a regular monthly basis by estimating the yearly cost and determining the monthly amount needed to be set aside for that expense. A helpful formula is to allow the previous year's expense and add 5 percent.

	Estimated Cost	Per Month
1. Vacation	$ _____ ÷ 12 =	$ _____
2. Dentist	$ _____ ÷ 12 =	$ _____
3. Doctor	$ _____ ÷ 12 =	$ _____
4. Automobile	$ _____ ÷ 12 =	$ _____
5. Annual Insurance	$ _____ ÷ 12 =	$ _____
(Life)	($ _____ ÷ 12 =	$ _____)
(Health)	($ _____ ÷ 12 =	$ _____)
(Auto)	($ _____ ÷ 12 =	$ _____)
(Home)	($ _____ ÷ 12 =	$ _____)
6. Clothing	$ _____ ÷ 12 =	$ _____
7. Investments	$ _____ ÷ 12 =	$ _____
8. Other	$ _____ ÷ 12 =	$ _____
	$ _____ ÷ 12 =	$ _____

VARIABLE EXPENSE PLANNING

Plan for those expenses that are not paid on a regular monthly basis by estimating the yearly cost and determining the monthly amount needed to be set aside for that expense. A helpful formula is to allow the previous year's expense and add 5 percent.

	Estimated Cost	Per Month
1. Vacation	$ _____ ÷ 12 =	$ _____
2. Dentist	$ _____ ÷ 12 =	$ _____
3. Doctor	$ _____ ÷ 12 =	$ _____
4. Automobile	$ _____ ÷ 12 =	$ _____
5. Annual Insurance	$ _____ ÷ 12 =	$ _____
(Life)	($ _____ ÷ 12 =	$ _____)
(Health)	($ _____ ÷ 12 =	$ _____)
(Auto)	($ _____ ÷ 12 =	$ _____)
(Home)	($ _____ ÷ 12 =	$ _____)
6. Clothing	$ _____ ÷ 12 =	$ _____
7. Investments	$ _____ ÷ 12 =	$ _____
8. Other	$ _____ ÷ 12 =	$ _____
	$ _____ ÷ 12 =	$ _____

FORM 2

VARIABLE EXPENSE PLANNING

Plan for those expenses that are not paid on a regular monthly basis by estimating the yearly cost and determining the monthly amount needed to be set aside for that expense. A helpful formula is to allow the previous year's expense and add 5 percent.

	Estimated Cost	Per Month
1. Vacation	$ _____ ÷ 12 =	$ _____
2. Dentist	$ _____ ÷ 12 =	$ _____
3. Doctor	$ _____ ÷ 12 =	$ _____
4. Automobile	$ _____ ÷ 12 =	$ _____
5. Annual Insurance	$ _____ ÷ 12 =	$ _____
(Life)	($ _____ ÷ 12 =	$ _____)
(Health)	($ _____ ÷ 12 =	$ _____)
(Auto)	($ _____ ÷ 12 =	$ _____)
(Home)	($ _____ ÷ 12 =	$ _____)
6. Clothing	$ _____ ÷ 12 =	$ _____
7. Investments	$ _____ ÷ 12 =	$ _____
8. Other	$ _____ ÷ 12 =	$ _____
	$ _____ ÷ 12 =	$ _____

BUDGET PERCENTAGE GUIDELINES

Salary for guideline = $_____/year[1]

Gross Income Per Month $_____

1. Tithe	(___% of Gross)	(_____)	= $ _____
2. Tax	(___% of Gross)	(_____)	= $ _____

Net Spendable Income $_____

3. Housing	(___% of Net)	(_____)	= $ _____
4. Food	(___% of Net)	(_____)	= $ _____
5. Auto	(___% of Net)	(_____)	= $ _____
6. Insurance	(___% of Net)	(_____)	= $ _____
7. Debts	(___% of Net)	(_____)	= $ _____
8. Enter./Rec.	(___% of Net)	(_____)	= $ _____
9. Clothing	(___% of Net)	(_____)	= $ _____
10. Savings	(___% of Net)	(_____)	= $ _____
11. Medical	(___% of Net)	(_____)	= $ _____
12. Miscellaneous	(___% of Net)	(_____)	= $ _____
13. Education	(___% of Net)	(_____)	= $ _____
14. Investments	(___% of Net)	(_____)	= $ _____

Total (Cannot exceed Net Spendable Income) $ _____

15. Unallocated Surplus Income   (____N/A____) = $ _____

1. Refer to page 37 for percentage guidelines.

FORM 3

BUDGET PERCENTAGE GUIDELINES

Salary for guideline = $_____/year[1]

Gross Income Per Month $_____

1. Tithe	(___% of Gross)	(_____)	= $ _____
2. Tax	(___% of Gross)	(_____)	= $ _____

Net Spendable Income $_____

3. Housing	(___% of Net)	(_____)	= $ _____
4. Food	(___% of Net)	(_____)	= $ _____
5. Auto	(___% of Net)	(_____)	= $ _____
6. Insurance	(___% of Net)	(_____)	= $ _____
7. Debts	(___% of Net)	(_____)	= $ _____
8. Enter./Rec.	(___% of Net)	(_____)	= $ _____
9. Clothing	(___% of Net)	(_____)	= $ _____
10. Savings	(___% of Net)	(_____)	= $ _____
11. Medical	(___% of Net)	(_____)	= $ _____
12. Miscellaneous	(___% of Net)	(_____)	= $ _____
13. Education	(___% of Net)	(_____)	= $ _____
14. Investments	(___% of Net)	(_____)	= $ _____

Total (Cannot exceed Net Spendable Income) $ _____

15. Unallocated Surplus Income   (___N/A___) = $ _____

1. Refer to page 37 for percentage guidelines.

FORM 3

BUDGET ANALYSIS

Per Year $_____

Per Month $_____

Net Spendable Income
Per Month $_____

MONTHLY PAYMENT CATEGORY	EXISTING BUDGET	MONTHLY GUIDELINE BUDGET	DIFFERENCE + OR -	NEW MONTHLY BUDGET
1. Tithe				
2. Tax				
Net Spendable Income (per month)	$_____	$_____	$_____	$_____
3. Housing				
4. Food				
5. Auto				
6. Insurance				
7. Debts				
8. Enter./Recreation				
9. Clothing				
10. Savings				
11. Medical				
12. Miscellaneous				
13. Education				
14. Investments				
Totals (Items 3-14)	$_____	$_____	////////	$_____

15. Unallocated Surplus Income				

FORM 4

BUDGET ANALYSIS

Per Year $_____

Per Month $_____

Net Spendable Income
Per Month $_____

MONTHLY PAYMENT CATEGORY	EXISTING BUDGET	MONTHLY GUIDELINE BUDGET	DIFFERENCE + OR -	NEW MONTHLY BUDGET
1. Tithe				
2. Tax				
Net Spendable Income (per month)	$_____	$_____	$_____	$_____
3. Housing				
4. Food				
5. Auto				
6. Insurance				
7. Debts				
8. Enter./Recreation				
9. Clothing				
10. Savings				
11. Medical				
12. Miscellaneous				
13. Education				
14. Investments				
Totals (Items 3-14)	$_____	$_____		$_____

15. Unallocated Surplus Income				

FORM 4

BUDGET ANALYSIS

Per Year $_____

Per Month $_____

Net Spendable Income
Per Month $_____

MONTHLY PAYMENT CATEGORY	EXISTING BUDGET	MONTHLY GUIDELINE BUDGET	DIFFERENCE + OR -	NEW MONTHLY BUDGET
1. Tithe				
2. Tax				
Net Spendable Income (per month)	$_____	$_____	$_____	$_____
3. Housing				
4. Food				
5. Auto				
6. Insurance				
7. Debts				
8. Enter./Recreation				
9. Clothing				
10. Savings				
11. Medical				
12. Miscellaneous				
13. Education				
14. Investments				
Totals (Items 3-14)	$_____	$_____	////////	$_____

15. Unallocated Surplus Income				

FORM 4

BUDGET ANALYSIS

Per Year $_____

Per Month $_____

Net Spendable Income
Per Month $_____

MONTHLY PAYMENT CATEGORY	EXISTING BUDGET	MONTHLY GUIDELINE BUDGET	DIFFERENCE + OR -	NEW MONTHLY BUDGET
1. Tithe				
2. Tax				
Net Spendable Income (per month)	$_____	$_____	$_____	$_____
3. Housing				
4. Food				
5. Auto				
6. Insurance				
7. Debts				
8. Enter./Recreation				
9. Clothing				
10. Savings				
11. Medical				
12. Miscellaneous				
13. Education				
14. Investments				
Totals (Items 3-14)	$_____	$_____	/////////	$_____

15. Unallocated Surplus Income				

FORM 4

INCOME ALLOCATION

INCOME		INCOME SOURCE/PAY PERIOD			
BUDGET CATEGORY	MONTHLY ALLOCATION				
1. Tithe					
2. Tax					
3. Housing					
4. Food					
5. Auto					
6. Insurance					
7. Debts					
8. Enter./Recreation					
9. Clothing					
10. Savings					
11. Medical					
12. Miscellaneous					
13. Education					
14. Investments					
15. Unallocated Surplus Income					

FORM 5

INCOME ALLOCATION

INCOME		INCOME SOURCE/PAY PERIOD			
BUDGET CATEGORY	MONTHLY ALLOCATION				
1. Tithe					
2. Tax					
3. Housing					
4. Food					
5. Auto					
6. Insurance					
7. Debts					
8. Enter./Recreation					
9. Clothing					
10. Savings					
11. Medical					
12. Miscellaneous					
13. Education					
14. Investments					
15. Unallocated Surplus Income					

INCOME ALLOCATION

		INCOME SOURCE/PAY PERIOD			
INCOME					
BUDGET CATEGORY	MONTHLY ALLOCATION				
1. Tithe					
2. Tax					
3. Housing					
4. Food					
5. Auto					
6. Insurance					
7. Debts					
8. Enter./Recreation					
9. Clothing					
10. Savings					
11. Medical					
12. Miscellaneous					
13. Education					
14. Investments					
15. Unallocated Surplus Income					

FORM 5

INCOME ALLOCATION

INCOME		INCOME SOURCE/PAY PERIOD			
BUDGET CATEGORY	MONTHLY ALLOCATION				
1. Tithe					
2. Tax					
3. Housing					
4. Food					
5. Auto					
6. Insurance					
7. Debts					
8. Enter./Recreation					
9. Clothing					
10. Savings					
11. Medical					
12. Miscellaneous					
13. Education					
14. Investments					
15. Unallocated Surplus Income					

SAVINGS ACCOUNT ALLOCATIONS

Date	Deposit	With-drawal	Balance	Housing	Food	Auto Insur.	Auto Maint.	Insur-ance	Clothes	Medical					

FORM 6

SAVINGS ACCOUNT ALLOCATIONS

Date	Deposit	With-drawal	Balance	Housing	Food	Auto Insur.	Auto Maint.	Insur-ance	Clothes	Medical				

FORM 6

SAVINGS ACCOUNT ALLOCATIONS

Date	Deposit	With-drawal	Balance	Housing	Food	Auto Insur.	Auto Maint.	Insur-ance	Clothes	Medical					

FORM 6

SAVINGS ACCOUNT ALLOCATIONS

Date	Deposit	With-drawal	Balance	Housing	Food	Auto Insur.	Auto Maint.	Insur-ance	Clothes	Medical

FORM 6

SAVINGS ACCOUNT ALLOCATIONS

Date	Deposit	With-drawal	Balance	Housing	Food	Auto Insur.	Auto Maint.	Insur-ance	Clothes	Medical					

FORM 6

SAVINGS ACCOUNT ALLOCATIONS

Date	Deposit	With-drawal	Balance	Housing	Food	Auto Insur.	Auto Maint.	Insur-ance	Clothes	Medical	

FORM 6

INDIVIDUAL ACCOUNT PAGE

_____ $ _____ $ _____
ACCOUNT CATEGORY   ALLOCATION   ALLOCATION

DATE	TRANSACTION	DEPOSIT		WITHDRAWAL		BALANCE	

FORM 7

INDIVIDUAL ACCOUNT PAGE

ACCOUNT CATEGORY $ _____ ALLOCATION $ _____ ALLOCATION

DATE	TRANSACTION	DEPOSIT		WITHDRAWAL		BALANCE	

INDIVIDUAL ACCOUNT PAGE

ACCOUNT CATEGORY	$ ALLOCATION	$ ALLOCATION

DATE	TRANSACTION	DEPOSIT	WITHDRAWAL	BALANCE

FORM 7

INDIVIDUAL ACCOUNT PAGE

ACCOUNT CATEGORY	$ ALLOCATION	$ ALLOCATION

DATE	TRANSACTION	DEPOSIT	WITHDRAWAL	BALANCE

FORM 7

INDIVIDUAL ACCOUNT PAGE

$ _____ $ _____

_____ ACCOUNT CATEGORY   ALLOCATION   ALLOCATION

DATE	TRANSACTION	DEPOSIT		WITHDRAWAL		BALANCE	

FORM 7

INDIVIDUAL ACCOUNT PAGE

	_____	$ _____		$ _____	
	ACCOUNT CATEGORY	ALLOCATION		ALLOCATION	

DATE	TRANSACTION	DEPOSIT	WITHDRAWAL	BALANCE

FORM 7

INDIVIDUAL ACCOUNT PAGE

	$		$	
ACCOUNT CATEGORY	ALLOCATION		ALLOCATION	

DATE	TRANSACTION	DEPOSIT	WITHDRAWAL	BALANCE

FORM 7

INDIVIDUAL ACCOUNT PAGE

$ _____ $ _____

_____   ALLOCATION   ALLOCATION
ACCOUNT CATEGORY

DATE	TRANSACTION	DEPOSIT		WITHDRAWAL		BALANCE	

FORM 7

INDIVIDUAL ACCOUNT PAGE

_____ ACCOUNT CATEGORY	$ _____ ALLOCATION	$ _____ ALLOCATION		

DATE	TRANSACTION	DEPOSIT	WITHDRAWAL	BALANCE

FORM 7

INDIVIDUAL ACCOUNT PAGE

ACCOUNT CATEGORY $ _____ ALLOCATION $ _____ ALLOCATION

DATE	TRANSACTION	DEPOSIT	WITHDRAWAL	BALANCE

FORM 7

INDIVIDUAL ACCOUNT PAGE

		$ _____	$ _____
	ACCOUNT CATEGORY	ALLOCATION	ALLOCATION

DATE	TRANSACTION	DEPOSIT		WITHDRAWAL		BALANCE	

FORM 7

INDIVIDUAL ACCOUNT PAGE

		$		$	
	ACCOUNT CATEGORY	ALLOCATION		ALLOCATION	

DATE	TRANSACTION	DEPOSIT		WITHDRAWAL		BALANCE	

FORM 7

INDIVIDUAL ACCOUNT PAGE

| | ACCOUNT CATEGORY | | $ ALLOCATION | | $ ALLOCATION |

DATE	TRANSACTION	DEPOSIT		WITHDRAWAL		BALANCE	

FORM 7

INDIVIDUAL ACCOUNT PAGE

_____ $_____ $_____
ACCOUNT CATEGORY   ALLOCATION   ALLOCATION

DATE	TRANSACTION	DEPOSIT		WITHDRAWAL		BALANCE	

FORM 7

INDIVIDUAL ACCOUNT PAGE

ACCOUNT CATEGORY	$ ALLOCATION	$ ALLOCATION

DATE	TRANSACTION	DEPOSIT		WITHDRAWAL		BALANCE	

FORM 7

INDIVIDUAL ACCOUNT PAGE

	ACCOUNT CATEGORY	$ _____ ALLOCATION	$ _____ ALLOCATION

DATE	TRANSACTION	DEPOSIT		WITHDRAWAL		BALANCE	

FORM 7

INDIVIDUAL ACCOUNT PAGE

ACCOUNT CATEGORY $ _____ ALLOCATION $ _____ ALLOCATION

DATE	TRANSACTION	DEPOSIT	WITHDRAWAL	BALANCE

INDIVIDUAL ACCOUNT PAGE

ACCOUNT CATEGORY	$ ALLOCATION	$ ALLOCATION

DATE	TRANSACTION	DEPOSIT	WITHDRAWAL	BALANCE

FORM 7

INDIVIDUAL ACCOUNT PAGE

	ACCOUNT CATEGORY	$ ALLOCATION	$ ALLOCATION

DATE	TRANSACTION	DEPOSIT	WITHDRAWAL	BALANCE

FORM 7

INDIVIDUAL ACCOUNT PAGE

$ _____ $ _____

_____   ALLOCATION   ALLOCATION
ACCOUNT CATEGORY

DATE	TRANSACTION	DEPOSIT		WITHDRAWAL		BALANCE	

FORM 7

INDIVIDUAL ACCOUNT PAGE

ACCOUNT CATEGORY $ _____ ALLOCATION $ _____ ALLOCATION

DATE	TRANSACTION	DEPOSIT		WITHDRAWAL		BALANCE	

FORM 7

INDIVIDUAL ACCOUNT PAGE

ACCOUNT CATEGORY $_____ ALLOCATION $_____ ALLOCATION

DATE	TRANSACTION	DEPOSIT		WITHDRAWAL		BALANCE	

FORM 7

CHECKBOOK LEDGER

DATE	CK. #	TRANSACTION	DEPOSIT	WITHDRAWAL	BALANCE

FORM 7a

CHECKBOOK LEDGER

DATE	CK. #	TRANSACTION	DEPOSIT	WITHDRAWAL	BALANCE

FORM 7a

CHECKBOOK LEDGER

DATE	CK. #	TRANSACTION	DEPOSIT	WITHDRAWAL	BALANCE

FORM 7a

CHECKBOOK LEDGER

DATE	CK. #	TRANSACTION	DEPOSIT	WITHDRAWAL	BALANCE

FORM 7a

CHECKBOOK LEDGER

DATE	CK. #	TRANSACTION	DEPOSIT	WITHDRAWAL	BALANCE

FORM 7a

CHECKBOOK LEDGER

DATE	CK. #	TRANSACTION	DEPOSIT	WITHDRAWAL	BALANCE

FORM 7a

CHECKBOOK LEDGER

DATE	CK. #	TRANSACTION	DEPOSIT	WITHDRAWAL	BALANCE

FORM 7a

CHECKBOOK LEDGER

DATE	CK. #	TRANSACTION	DEPOSIT	WITHDRAWAL	BALANCE

FORM 7a

CHECKBOOK LEDGER

DATE	CK. #	TRANSACTION	DEPOSIT	WITHDRAWAL	BALANCE

CHECKBOOK LEDGER

DATE	CK. #	TRANSACTION		DEPOSIT		WITHDRAWAL		BALANCE	

FORM 7a

CHECKBOOK LEDGER

DATE	CK. #	TRANSACTION	DEPOSIT	WITHDRAWAL	BALANCE

FORM 7a

CHECKBOOK LEDGER

DATE	CK. #	TRANSACTION	DEPOSIT	WITHDRAWAL	BALANCE

FORM 7a

CHECKBOOK LEDGER

DATE	CK. #	TRANSACTION	DEPOSIT	WITHDRAWAL	BALANCE

FORM 7a

CHECKBOOK LEDGER

DATE	CK. #	TRANSACTION	DEPOSIT	WITHDRAWAL	BALANCE

FORM 7a

CHECKBOOK LEDGER

DATE	CK. #	TRANSACTION	DEPOSIT	WITHDRAWAL	BALANCE

FORM 7a

CHECKBOOK LEDGER

DATE	CK. #	TRANSACTION		DEPOSIT	WITHDRAWAL	BALANCE
			○			
			○			
			○			
			○			
			○			
			○			
			○			
			○			
			○			
			○			
			○			
			○			
			○			
			○			
			○			
			○			
			○			
			○			
			○			
			○			
			○			
			○			
			○			
			○			
			○			
			○			
			○			
			○			
			○			
			○			
			○			
			○			
			○			
			○			
			○			
			○			

FORM 7a

LIST OF DEBTS

as of _____

TO WHOM OWED	CONTACT NAME / PHONE NUMBER	PAY OFF	PAYMENTS LEFT	MONTHLY PAYMENT	DUE DATE

FORM 8

LIST OF DEBTS

as of _____

TO WHOM OWED	CONTACT NAME PHONE NUMBER	PAY OFF	PAYMENTS LEFT	MONTHLY PAYMENT	DUE DATE

FORM 8

LIST OF DEBTS

as of _____

TO WHOM OWED	CONTACT NAME PHONE NUMBER	PAY OFF	PAYMENTS LEFT	MONTHLY PAYMENT	DUE DATE

FORM 8

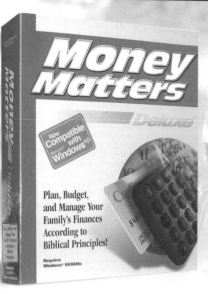

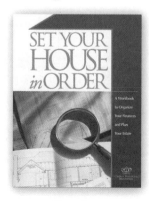